Original title:
Petals on the Windowsill

Copyright © 2025 Creative Arts Management OÜ
All rights reserved.

Author: Nathaniel Blackwood
ISBN HARDBACK: 978-1-80581-714-7
ISBN PAPERBACK: 978-1-80581-241-8
ISBN EBOOK: 978-1-80581-714-7

The Colorful Fragments of Morning

Bright hues dance in the light,
A dainty flower takes flight.
A bee buzzes with a grin,
'No bouquet can match my spin!'

The coffee pot starts to play,
With fragrant tunes to greet the day.
A squirrel darts, steals the show,
'Just me, your morning bro!'

Nature's Gentle Invitation

In the garden, a call is heard,
A sunflower winks, quite absurd.
'Join the fun, don't be a grouch,
We'll dance like leaves on the couch!'

Birds chirp jokes from up above,
Their harmony, a cheerful love.
Come sip dew, it's quite the treat,
With bugs that dance on tiny feet!

Blossoms in the Air

Fluttering friends on the breeze,
Giggles stirred by playful trees.
A butterfly flirts, raises a wing,
'Who needs a prince? I'm the real thing!'

The daisies twist in the sun,
They laugh aloud, oh what fun!
Whispers of color, scents combine,
As nature craves a glass of wine!

Memories Resting on the Ledge

A tiny pot holds tales untold,
Of mischief, laughter, and marigold.
'Not just decor, we're stories bright,
You can't keep us down; we're a thrilling sight!'

Time ticks on, the sun sets low,
In cozy nooks, the petals glow.
Just one wish whispered in gloom,
'A dance with dust bunnies in the room!'

Splendid Views of Impermanence

Bright blooms dance in the breeze,
A show for all—except the bees.
They buzz around in silly glee,
"Hurry up! Come look at me!"

But just like them, these colors fade,
A whimsical parade is made.
Gone tomorrow, but who would mind?
New laughs and giggles we will find.

Curled Around the Edges

A curl upon the sill so fine,
It seems to joke with morning wine.
They tease the birds to come and see,
"Hey, look at our green comedy!"

While wind blows tricks and leaves a laugh,
They wriggle like a silly calf.
Must be the game of sun and shade,
A hilarious world they have made.

Flutters of a Whispering Wand

A flutter by the window frames,
Whispers of nature, silly claims.
"The sun is ticklish! Can't you see?"
"Join our giggles, you'll feel free!"

Frogs in the bushes croak a tune,
And dance beneath the laughing moon.
Even the flowers prance and play,
As they wave goodbye to the day.

The Quiet Serenade of Nature

Nature hums a gentle song,
Where quirky things just can't be wrong.
A leaf that lands on top of a cat,
"Hey, look at me! I'm quite the brat!"

A sneeze from grass, it sets off glee,
While ants organize a comedy spree.
With every chuckle, a new day starts,
In this riot of colors, we find our hearts.

The Poetry of Softness

Whispers of color, bright and bold,
Lazily draped as if they're gold.
They giggle and sway in a playful dance,
Chasing the bees, oh what a chance!

Sunlight spills laughter, such a delight,
Tickling leaves, oh what a sight.
They've got a secret, that cheeky bloom,
Practicing winks in their cozy room.

A breeze joins in, oh what a tease,
Kissing the petals, just to please.
Daring the squirrel to join the fun,
Under the sky, they bask in the sun.

Even the raindrops wish to play,
As they drum on branches, come what may.
Nature's joke, a sight to behold,
In this soft world, laughter unfolds.

A Story in Every Shade

Crimson laughs and yellow grins,
They spin wild tales on gentle winds.
Orange dreams and blue delights,
Whisper secrets through sunny nights.

Each color giggles, weaving a thread,
In soft conversations, softly said.
They plot mischief with each little sway,
A riot of stories in playful array.

Green buds gossip, "What's this attire?"
"Ten shades of mischief, never tire!"
They burst with giggles, a colorful spree,
In a world where hues flee the ordinary.

At dusk, they burst into cheeky cheer,
Bidding farewell to the day's frontier.
With every wink, they sketch a tale,
In hues of laughter, they shall prevail.

Hues of Life's Ephemeral Nature

Fleeting moments wrapped in pastel shades,
Life's little circus in peppy parades.
They dance like marionettes on strings,
This art of laughter, oh how it sings!

Each hue a giggle, a comic twist,
In the garden of jest, none can resist.
Rainbow mischief under the sun,
Life's brief joys, oh, what fun!

Here comes the moon, a big round grin,
Painting the night where stories begin.
It winks at the flowers, "Let's have a ball!"
In this world of whimsy, we welcome all!

Every moment flutters with joy,
Kicking the dust, like a playful toy.
For life's vibrant jest, let's raise a cheer,
In colors and laughter, we hold so dear!

The Quiet Reminder of Life's Beauty

A bloom peeks in, oh so sly,
It nods at me, with no goodbye.
I chuckle at its sneaky flair,
Reminding me spring doesn't care.

A squirrel hops by, full of glee,
Thinking the petals are his tea.
He twirls around, so spry and bold,
Nature's antics, never old.

The sun streams in, a playful glow,
Fluffy clouds march on in tow.
Each flower whispers, quite absurd,
Life's beauty waits, not to be heard.

With every breeze, a giggle stirs,
A merry dance, the world prefers.
So smile, dear friend, let worries fly,
For each small bloom will wave goodbye!

A Gallery of Nature's Art

In the morning light, colors sway,
A canvas bright, in disarray.
The daisies strut in a grand show,
While butterflies glance, then just go.

With every hue, the frogs complain,
They croak their thoughts on the windowpane.
The daisies blush, the lilies laugh,
Nature's art is quite the gaffe.

Each petal sports a quirky grin,
As raindrops add a splash of whim.
A bumblebee, all dressed in stripes,
Can't figure out, just what's his type.

The breeze carries a silly tune,
As clouds join in, parade by noon.
A gallery where laughter reigns,
Just look and see the playful gains!

Gentle Remnants of Wandering Thoughts

A stray thought floats, like a seed,
Drifting on a breeze, with speed.
It lands among the cheerful blooms,
Who giggle soft in their perfume.

Each moment slips, a fleeting glance,
The daisies dance a silly dance.
With every rustle, they conspire,
To make one laugh, never tire.

Bright colors tease my sleepy mind,
As busy bees hum, unconfined.
I chase a laugh, but it runs fast,
In nature's games, I'm often last.

So here I sit with thoughts that play,
As flowers giggle in their way.
The beauty hides in every wink,
Just pause a second, share a drink!

Fragrant Memories in the Air

The breeze arrives with scents galore,
Bringing tales from the garden floor.
A whiff of mint, a hint of thyme,
These fragrant memories stir in rhyme.

Oh, how the daisies tease the bees,
With catchy tunes and swaying knees.
A wacky dance ensues in flight,
Nature's jesters, pure delight.

Each bloom a letter, lightly penned,
A funny story with no end.
They whisper secrets in delight,
And share their laugh in morning light.

As petals flutter, a lively cheer,
They celebrate life, year after year.
So sniff and smile, and let them share,
These fragrant laughs, light as air!

Echoes of Spring's Forgotten Hues

A daffodil tried to tell a joke,
But all it did was make me choke.
Its neighbors giggled, petals aglow,
Wondering where all the good bees go.

On a sunny day, a tulip sneezed,
Causing a ruckus, as it pleased.
The daisies laughed, they fell in a heap,
While the roses snored like they were asleep.

The sun shone bright, a bee flew by,
Winking at me with a curious eye.
I tossed a crumb, oh what a sight,
It danced in circles, till it took flight.

Yet evening comes with laughter and sighs,
As colors fade and night draws nigh.
We'll recall these blooms from far and wide,
In gardens where laughter and chaos collide.

The Beauty of Things Left Behind

A shoe was left by the garden gate,
It startled a squirrel, who ran, quite irate.
Old gloves lay resting against a rose,
Debating their fate, as weeds overgrow.

Forgotten hats have taken a stance,
On branches above, they sway and dance.
Each flapping brim tells a story grand,
Of windswept dreams in a pixie land.

The garden gnome starts to bust a move,
With every stray breeze, he starts to groove.
He gives a wink to a flower or two,
As if proclaiming, 'This party's for you!'

Well-trodden paths are paved with delight,
Where laughter blooms, and shadows take flight.
In the beauty of things left to chance,
Life finds a way to spark a romance.

A Fragrant Farewell at Twilight

In the fading light, a lavender wave,
Whispers sweet secrets, bold and brave.
It tickles my nose as the birds take flight,
Singing goodbye to the day, what a sight!

A rosemary sprig tried to tell a tale,
But ended up snagged on a passing snail.
They debated paths and who's really slow,
With laughter erupting, stealing the show.

As night descends with a starry wink,
The parsley giggles, pushing me to think.
What makes the world spin, while we just stop?
A fragrant farewell that'll never drop.

So let's toast the dusk with a chuckle or two,
To the herbs and blooms, and the fun they woo.
In the garden of spirits, let laughter swell,
As we bid farewell with an aromatic spell.

Secrets of the Blooming Season

Underneath the blooms, a secret crew,
Of ladybugs plotting, who just flew.
They take their time with a gossiping spree,
While daisies nod in amused harmony.

A shy little violet, with a wink,
Shared her gossip but forgot to think.
Soon, all the tulips joined in the jest,
While the sunflowers swayed, putting them to the test.

The cheerful marigold had the best lines,
Telling tales of sunbeams, with bright designs.
Each petal adorned with laughter's embrace,
In the garden, joy found its place.

So let's tiptoe through this flowery domain,
Where giggles bloom, and no vibes are plain.
In the secrets kept, amid green and gold,
Is laughter the magic we need to uphold?

A Tapestry of Bloom

Bright blooms dance with the breeze,
They giggle, swaying with ease.
A bee buzzes in a grand ballet,
Whispering secrets in a playful way.

A sunbeam tickles a rose in jest,
While daisies challenge who's the best.
Laughter bursts from a clumsy ant,
Tripping over its own little plant.

Colors clash like a paint fight,
Every shade laughing, vibrant and bright.
Nature's pranksters, bold and free,
Creating chaos, just wait and see!

In this garden, fun never ends,
Where flowers dance and joy ascends.
With petals that twirl and twine,
A tapestry of bloom, oh so divine!

Fragrance of Forgotten Gardens

In a garden where the weeds tell jokes,
Roses snicker at the silly folks.
A daffodil performs a wacky jig,
While mushrooms sip tea—quite big!

Sunflowers wink with their golden eyes,
Plotting schemes beneath the skies.
A shy lilac blushes, feeling bold,
Spilling secrets of old loves told.

Lettuce laughs at its own green hue,
Saying, 'Why not add a flower or two?'
With each whiff of zany delight,
The forgotten garden sparks into light!

So come and join this floral spree,
Where every blossom laughs with glee.
In fragrant air, worries unwind,
A giggly pleasure, so well-defined!

Echoes of a Floral Daydream

In a daydream filled with bloom,
A tulip sneezes, causing a boom!
Petals scatter with a plushy plop,
Roses giggle, 'Let's never stop!'

A violet painted with polka dots,
Tells tales of wiggly garden spots.
The lilies leap, feeling sprightly,
Swaying gently, ever so lightly.

Bumblebees, the gossiping crew,
Buzz about the freshest dew.
They share laughs of a garden plot,
Making memories that won't be forgot.

As sunlight filters through each bloom,
Laughter echoes, dispelling gloom.
In this daydream of vibrant hue,
Floral joy reigns, always anew!

Sunlight Through Delicate Leaves

Sunlight dances through leafy greens,
Whispering secrets in bright sheens.
Each leaf a comedian, ever so spry,
Tickling the winds as they flutter by.

Buds make jokes in the morning rays,
Spinning tales of silly plays.
With the breeze as their merry muse,
They all laugh at their own funny views.

A sunflower shouts, 'I'm the tallest here!'
While daisies claim, 'We're flawless, my dear!'
The laughter rings, a sweet refrain,
In this realm where joy is plain.

As sunlight shines through each design,
The garden chuckles, purely divine.
With each new sunrise, the humor weaves,
A tapestry of laughter among the leaves!

A Window Framed in Color

A curious sprout poked its head,
On the sill, it danced instead.
While the sun peered through the glass,
It wobbled like a clown with sass.

Bees whispered jokes in the breeze,
Teasing blooms with such great ease.
"Why don't flowers have a car?"
"Because they can't drive very far!"

A sunflower tried to take a leap,
But tripped and fell into a heap.
The paintbrush sky let out a giggle,
As the daffodils wobbled and wiggled.

Laughter echoed from the ground,
As petals tossed and spun around.
In this nook, where colors sprout,
Life's a comedy, without a doubt!

Serenading Shadows

In the twilight, shadows creep,
Bouncing to a rhythm deep.
A violet wink and a daisy grin,
Join the party, let the fun begin!

They twirl and sway in a merry dance,
A humorous chance for a sprouting romance.
"Why are we just shadows?" one cried,
"Because light's playing peekaboo, we can't hide!"

A laugh rang out from a silly fern,
"Let's boogie till the sun's return!"
Chased by giggles, the moon did flee,
As the flowers declared, "Come join the spree!"

With their laughter fading into night,
The shadows reveled in sheer delight.
In this whimsical, giggling show,
Every corner had a twinkling glow!

Hues of Hope and Longing

A redbud dreamed of sky-high flights,
While a dandelion practiced its heights.
"I'll float away on a whim," it said,
"Just need a breeze and a soft bed!"

Colorful whispers brushed the air,
At the heart of dreams, they'd freely share.
"Why do we reach for the sun so high?"
"Because up there, we can touch the sky!"

A sunflower sighed, "I'm stuck down here,
Why can't I be a bird, I fear!"
But the daisies laughed, "Oh, dear friend,
Just rise in spirit, the fun won't end!"

Amidst the blooms, a chuckle flew,
In the hues of hope, the joy just grew.
From longing hearts and laughter's chime,
They found their joy in rhythm and rhyme!

The Last Smile of Summer

As summer waved its final kiss,
The blooms giggled, perfect bliss.
"Who's ready for a grand goodbye?"
Asked the daisies in a sunny sigh.

They held a party, bright and bold,
With stories of warmth that never grows old.
"What's the silliest joke we can find?"
"Why did the flower feel so blind?"

"Because bright light made it squint its eyes!
That's why it started to improvise!"
They chuckled, twirling in the fading light,
Spilling laughter on the approaching night.

With a laugh, they joined in tune,
Bidding farewell to the warm afternoon.
In the twilight, their joy would shimmer,
As they savored the last smile, forever glimmer!

Splashed with Softness

Fluffy clouds in the sky,
Rained a bit too much pie.
Splashed on my sunny face,
Oh, what a messy place!

Socks turned rainbow delight,
Splatters of silly sight.
Dancing in puddles new,
Laughing, who knew we'd brew!

Giggling as we fall down,
Wearing mud like a crown.
Chasing dreams on a whim,
With each giggle, we swim.

Sunshine peeking through cheer,
Forget the clouds, let's steer.
With laughter all around,
Joy and silliness abound!

The Remains of Joyful Whispers

In the cupboard, whispers hide,
Cookies left to abide.
A crumb trail leads us there,
To giggles in the air!

Teacups crashing on the floor,
Oh, what a raucous chore!
But laughter's the recipe,
For fun, it's quite a spree.

Whispers turn to merry shouts,
Forget the worries and doubts.
With each clink we toast,
To those who love us most!

Candles flicker, shadows dance,
Life is one big, silly prance.
Nothing serious to dwell,
Just laughter, can't you tell?

Petals of a Wistful Tale

Once a flower wore a hat,
It looked quite silly, don't you chat?
Bobbing here and swinging there,
Tickling bees without a care!

Hats and blooms began to twirl,
Every gust made petals whirl.
Giggling in floral glee,
Nature's jester, wild and free!

Silly dancers in the breeze,
Tickling toes of buzzing bees.
Each petal a story spun,
Under the warm, bright sun!

Life of blossoms, laughter's cheer,
Budding dreams are growing near.
Lasting tales in every shade,
In this garden, joy is made!

The Ebb and Flow of Beauty

Like waves, we dance and sway,
Chasing worries far away.
A tangle of silly mane,
Who needs calm when you've got rain?

Laughter lingers in the air,
Bouncing here without a care.
The tide brings laughter, oh dear,
Splashing friends, we're filled with cheer!

Breezy whispers through the trees,
Swaying couples, feeling free.
The rhythm of joy in flight,
Guides us through the starry night!

Floating on clouds of delight,
Life's a party, pure and bright.
With each wave, more giggles flow,
In this dance, joy's the show!

Charms of the Window's Light

A flower in bloom, it greets the sun,
Yet dances like it's just begun.
With a wobble and giggle, it sways in glee,
"Look at me, I'm the star of the spree!"

The light tickles petals, what a delight,
They shimmer and shine, oh what a sight!
But the cat walks by, drops a clumsy paw,
Now it's a game of who saw what flaw!

Buzzing bees come, looking for fun,
Sipping sweet nectar like they've just won.
But they trip and they tumble, in quite a mess,
Leaving the blossoms in sheer distress!

Laughing at the antics, the breeze has its say,
Whispers to flowers in a playful way.
"Join the circus!" it calls, "Let the show begin,
With a flick and a flutter, you'll surely win!"

The Call of the Untouched Blossoms

Alone by the curtain, they sit so proud,
Waiting for something they can show aloud.
"Are we not lovely?" they ask with a sigh,
"Why does no one stop as they pass by?"

Then a squirrel appears, eyes wide with fun,
"Hey flowers, let's play! Just let's run!"
He bounces and pounces, wiggling his tail,
"A game of peekaboo, let's set the trail!"

The sunlight giggles, causing quite a fuss,
As leaves start to rustle, making quite a bus.
"Bet you can't catch me!" the breeze seems to shout,
Sending petals swirling, round about!

At last, a child comes, with laughter so bright,
"Look at those flowers, they're soft, what a sight!"
They rustle with joy as the petals take flight,
Together they dance in the warm golden light!

Whispers of Flora at Dawn

Dawn breaks gently, with a soft silly grin,
The blossoms are yawning, ready to spin.
"Good morning, old sun, let's shake off the dew,
We're blooming and giggling, how about you?"

A snail slides in, moving oh so slow,
"Hey folks, did I miss the morning show?"
"It's starting right now!" the daisies reply,
As they twirl and twinkle, reaching for the sky.

The shadows are stretching, playing peek-a-boo,
While butterflies flutter with a splash of hue.
But the clumsy old bee, in his rush to appear,
Knocks over a bloom, causing great cheer!

"Oops! Apologies!" buzzed the bee with flair,
"Didn't mean to send your hat into the air!"
But the flowers just chuckle, as silly as can be,
Each whisper of laughter dances on the breeze!

Dreams Caught in Sunlight

In a sunny spot where the humor is thick,
The flowers plot pranks, each one a quick flick.
"Let's drop our seeds on the passerby,
And giggle together as they wonder why!"

Some spread their fragrance, oh what a tease,
While others just sway with the gentlest breeze.
"Here comes the gardener, let's hide for a bit!
We'll jump out and scare him, it'll be a hit!"

As the sun shines down, they twinkle with glee,
Dreams of mischief dancing wild and free.
With laughter and sunlight, the day is just right,
For flowers that know how to party all night!

So toast to the blossoms, each colorful friend,
With joy in their petals that never will end.
In a world of bright colors, they'll always shine,
Catching all sunshine, like bubbles of wine!

The Gentle Art of Letting Go

A flower waved goodbye with flair,
It opened wide but lost its hair.
"I'm free! I'm free!" it sang aloud,
While the wind turned it into a cloud.

The gardener sighed, an exasperated gaze,
"I watered you well, what's with the craze?"
Petals danced off, a wild parade,
Leaving a pot that looked quite dismayed.

The vase now holds a single sprout,
Next week it too might take a route.
Watch for the escape artist on the shelf,
A rogue plant choosing its life itself.

Echoes from a Forgotten Garden

In a corner where weeds play hide and seek,
A gnome snores loudly, oh what a cheek!
A daisy tried to wake the poor guy,
But his nap was grand under the blue sky.

The carrots conspired, "Let's give him a fright!"
A parade of ants danced into the night.
When he awoke, his hat in a twist,
He muttered, "I really should add this to my list."

Blossoms giggled with dewdrops on cheeks,
Letting the sun play peek-a-boo streaks.
A sprout in the back waved, looking dapper,
"Join the party, it's all just a caper!"

Stories Held in Quiet Corners

Once in a pot, an old cactus sighed,
"I've seen it all, I'm a legend worldwide."
A floppy fern laughed, responding with glee,
"What's the best story? Do tell it to me!"

"Oh, the time I pricked a man's nose so green,
He swore at the plants and fled from the scene!
I laughed and I laughed, it was such a hoot,
He learned plants aren't really made for a loot!"

The geranium smirked, "I'm better, you know,
I once swayed my way into a garden show!"
Cactus rolled eyes, "A show? How quaint!
While I, my dear friend, am a prickly saint!"

Colors That Breathe

Orange and yellow had a blowout fight,
"Too bright!" yelled green, "I'm losing my sight!"
Blue tried to calm them, but tripped on a hue,
"Stop all this shouting; I'm blue just for you!"

In the midst of chaos, a splash of pink stood,
Saying, "Why so serious? Let's brighten the mood!"
With a wink, neon joined in the display,
"Let's all just groove, it's a colorful day!"

They painted the fence, splattering joy,
Making a mess, oh what a ploy!
A rainbow appeared, laughter galore,
In gardens of fun, they danced evermore.

Nature's Soliloquy

A grasshopper plays the banjo, tight,
While squirrels dance under the pale moonlight.
The daisies gossip, they whisper and tease,
While bees drone on about their honeyed bees.

The clouds wear hats and giggle with glee,
As ants march in line, they're planning a spree.
A deer rolls its eyes at a butterfly's flit,
Nature's antics, oh how they fit!

With every raindrop, there's laughter around,
The frog's a comedian, with leaps that astound.
Flowers are jesters in technicolor hues,
Painting the garden with vibrant amuse.

Under the arches of vibrant sunbeams,
The rooster proclaims in comical dreams.
Nature chuckles as it spins and it twirls,
The world is a stage, a canvas that whirls.

A Palette of Hidden Dreams

In hues of laughter, the sun breaks the morn,
With playful breezes, all troubles are shorn.
The tulips are tickled by whispers of joy,
As they dance to the tunes that the swallows employ.

A dandelion wishes on fancies so bright,
While a bumblebee swerves, an erratic flight.
With brushes of color, the sky paints a grin,
And the trees sway their branches, as if to begin.

The clouds play peekaboo, hiding away,
While the sun throws petals in a silly display.
With every splash of blue, there's a chuckle to find,
The art of the day, oh so whimsically blind.

In a world where laughter and colors combine,
Every flower is witty, each leaf is divine.
A palette of dreams, oh what a delight,
As nature composes its whimsical sight.

Colors Riding the Wind

A balloon drifts up, like dreams in the air,
Chasing after rainbows and ribbons laid bare.
The wind whispers secrets, a giggle alight,
As kites flutter by, oh what a silly sight!

The daffodils sway, in a quirky ballet,
While a lazy cat naps, in the sun's warm sway.
Trees throw confetti, their leaves in a dance,
And a squirrel debates his next wild prance.

Colors spin 'round like a dizzying toy,
With butterflies laughing in purest of joy.
The sun plays hopscotch with shadows at play,
Each moment a quirk, in nature's cabaret.

So come join the party, let laughter unfurl,
In the midst of the garden, there's room for a whirl.
Colors riding on winds, both funny and grand,
A canvas of life, perfectly planned.

Sighs of the Sunlit Horizon

The sun, like a clown, peeks over the hills,
Tickling the daisies, igniting their thrills.
With a wink and a smile, it frolics around,
Spreading cheer to the earth, where laughter abounds.

The clouds exchange repartees, light as a feather,
As the breeze weaves stories of light-hearted weather.
A giggling brook runs, splashing pebbles with glee,
Chasing little fish that swim wild and free.

The horizon yawns wide, in hues all aglow,
While butterflies tumble, putting on quite the show.
The sun gives a sigh, in the glow of the day,
As nature celebrates in her own merry way.

So here in this haven, with joy all around,
The chorus of laughter is truly profound.
Sighs of delight, from the horizon so bright,
Remind us to cherish each whimsical sight.

Morning Breath of a Silent Room

The curtains yawn and stretch so wide,
Invasion of the sun, no place to hide.
A sock on the floor, a dance of dust,
I swear it winks! Oh, in it I trust.

The coffee's brewing, a fragrant tease,
It whispers sweet promises with ease.
My hair's a mess, yet I'm feeling bold,
Adventure awaits, or so I'm told.

A toast to the toast, too burnt on the side,
Laughter erupts, my breakfast pride!
I swipe crumbs off the floor with flair,
A culinary whirlwind, chaos in the air.

In this quiet room, where silence blooms,
Laughter and scents, they dance in the fumes.
Morning's gentle smile, it's a goofy show,
As I stumble through life, pretending to know.

The Hidden Language of Flowers

A sunflower grins, its humor bright,
While daisies gossip, oh what delight!
Roses blush, in a velvet gleam,
Whispering secrets, a flowery dream.

Tulips pretend in their fancy dress,
While violets giggle, no need to impress.
Dandelions puff, with a cheeky cheer,
Their seeds like wishes, drifting near.

Carnations quip, with a sassy stance,
'We're the life of the garden dance!'
In this floral chat, humor does bloom,
As I laugh with the bunch, in nature's room.

From petals to leaves, they share their glee,
In colors and scents so wild and free.
I'll take a wild guess, they plot and conspire,
To tickle our senses, with beauty they hire.

Soft Hues Against the Glass

The light streams in, on a lazy scene,
With colors that shimmer, oh what a sheen!
A butterfly flutters, right past the glass,
'How's it outside?' it seems to ask.

The window's adorned with a smudge or two,
Not quite a masterpiece, though it'll do.
A squirrel peeks in, with a fluffy tail,
Does it want nuts or just to regale?

Breezy whispers let giggles escape,
As shadows perform in their soft drape.
Each hue pokes fun, in a wink and a grin,
A cheerful reminder, let the day begin.

So here I sit, with a mug snug and warm,
Laughing at colors, who tease and charm.
Life at the window, a comedic play,
In shades of delight, brighten my day.

Simplicity in Fragile Beauty

A lone bloom stands, with a crooked stem,
It chuckles softly, 'Look, I'm a gem!'
The vase is crooked, oh what a sight,
Yet it wears its flaws, with sheer delight.

Breezes nudge, a playful push,
'Hold still!' they say, with a cheeky hush.
Droplets dance like they've found a tune,
While petals giggle, under the moon.

A bumblebee buzzes, with a jovial hum,
'Do I pertain, or have I come?'
The flower just laughs, 'You're part of the show,
Let's put on a party, together we'll grow!'

In each fragile blossom, a story unfolds,
With laughter and quirks, in colors of gold.
Simplicity reigns, as the fun stays in view,
Life's little jokes, in bloom's lovely hue.

The Weight of Fragile Wishes

Little dreams sit in a cup,
Frothy thoughts, oh what a mix!
They float and swirl, never give up,
Hoping for a sprinkle of tricks.

Each whimsy sighs with such delight,
Tickling the edge of my mind.
They dance around till the night,
As laughter and chaos unwind.

But whispers of wishes take flight,
In gatherings of soft delight,
They tumble and crash, oh what a sight,
Each moment a joke, pure and bright.

So I gather them up with a grin,
Pour them into a potion divine,
With a twist of fate, let the fun begin,
As whimsical worries intertwine.

Dawn's Sweet Embrace

Morning stretches, yawning wide,
Sunlight spills with silly glee,
The rooster crows, it's time to ride,
To breakfast land, oh tell me!

Pancakes dance like ballerinas,
Maple syrup glues the show,
Bananas wear their finest sheens,
While toast just somersaults below.

A giggle here, a chuckle there,
As orange juice plays hide and seek,
The coffee pot is my best prayer,
Caffeine brings laughter to the week!

So let's embrace this silly dawn,
With quirky bites, let's take our stake.
The world's a stage, we'll carry on,
In morning's bright and funny wake.

Unveiling Nature's Secrets

Nature whispers tales so neat,
In rustling leaves that groove and sway,
A squirrel skips, oh what a feat,
While flowers laugh and greet the day.

The earth is full of giggling streams,
That tickle rocks with bubbly cheer,
Each ripple ponders funny dreams,
Of frogs that sing for all to hear.

Bushes gossip, trees lean in,
Trading jokes, a secret spree,
Bees buzz by with goofy grins,
Spreading smiles from bumblebee.

So wander forth where laughter grows,
Amongst the ferns and nature's schemes,
For every secret that nature knows,
Is stuffed with joy and quirky dreams.

A Tincture of Calm

In a teacup filled with giggles,
The steam rises, a cheerful sigh,
Each sip tickles with little wiggles,
Stirring joy as the day goes by.

Fond memories float with gentle grace,
As spoons chat softly in their dance,
A splash of cream adds to the pace,
And sugar sprinkles a sweet romance.

Outside, the world may whirl and spin,
But here it's a calm, vibrant nook,
With laughter mixed in from within,
While the kettle gives one last look.

So sip away, let troubles melt,
In this cozy, funny retreat,
For in every cup, joy is felt,
As giggles and warmth sweetly greet.

The Echo of Soft Colors

Tiny blooms peek through the frames,
Whispers of laughter, teasing names.
They giggle in hues of pink and blue,
As the morning sun gives their antics cue.

Frolicsome flowers dance with flair,
Plotting mischief in the cool morning air.
A blossom declares, 'I'll steal the show!'
While another shouts, 'Well, let's go slow!'

They play hide and seek with the light,
Drawing smiles in the soft daylight.
Every wink, a colorful delight,
In a charming game that feels so right.

Tickled leaves, a fluttering tease,
Waving at birds, a feathered breeze.
Nature's jesters, cheerfully wild,
In a window wonderland, blissfully styled.

Blossoms Beckoning the Night

As twilight drapes a golden shawl,
The blooms invite the stars to sprawl.
'Come join our party!' they gladly cheer,
With petals that shimmer and twirl with beer.

A daisy proclaims, 'I can sing too!'
While rose rolls her eyes, 'Oh, how cute!'
They sway to a melody woven in dusk,
While daisies giggle and tulips musk.

'What a ruckus, oh what a view!'
'Is that really a star, or just old glue?'
They chuckle and shine, through the jasmine haze,
In a wild flower dance, they bask and blaze.

With moonlight drenching their fragile forms,
They spin and sway in soft floral storms.
Each petal and leaf a spark of glee,
In a midnight ballet, wild and free.

Nature's Songs in a Sunny Room

Sunlight streams, and what a sight,
A chorus of colors, pure delight!
The window swings wide with a cheeky grin,
Buds harmonizing, let the fun begin!

A tulip shouts, 'Could you hear that tune?'
While daisies dance around like a cartoon.
They rock to rhythms of soft, warm air,
Creating giggles everywhere, fair and square.

They plot a game of hit and miss,
While bumblebees hum, joining this bliss.
With petals bouncing on a sunlit floor,
The room's alive, who could ask for more?

In this bright space where laughter thrives,
That bloom in the corner truly derives.
A winking flower, whispering so cool,
Nature's jovial, sunlit school.

The Lament of Withering Beauty

Even the best can lose their flair,
A tulip sighed, 'Life's a breath of air.'
'Oh dear, look at me, all droopy and sad,'
Said one wilted bloom, considering the bad.

'Was it those bugs or the drought's brutal tease?
I swear I was vibrant, oh won't someone sneeze?'
While others chuckled, 'Let's not be blue,
Life is a giggle, more glee than rue.'

But lo and behold, what's that in the light?
A hummingbird flutters, oh what a sight!
'With a sip of nectar, your spirit shall rise,
You're not just a wallflower, darling, so wise!'

So together they laughed, crinkled and bold,
In the face of decay, their joy uncontrolled.
For what are the blooms but fleeting spark?
Funny how laughter can light up the dark.

The Calm After the Floral Storm

A flower dropped with such a plop,
My cat, upon it, chose to stop.
He sneezed and jumped with quite a flair,
As petals danced upon the air.

The vase now empty, what a sight,
The dog rolled in it with delight.
Chaos reigned, a colorful mess,
Who knew flowers could cause such stress?

Lily stuck to my shoe like glue,
As I walked, it took me two.
With each step, I left a trace,
Of floral elegance and disgrace.

So now we laugh, the pets and me,
A blooming circus, wild and free.
With every mishap, life's a dream,
In the calm, our laughter's the theme.

When Time Stops at the Bloom

The clock's not ticking, time's on pause,
As blooms begin to take their cause.
A bumblebee got snugly trapped,
In a flower's hug—how he yapped!

A toddler giggled, reached to grab,
The blooms that made the whole yard fab.
She slipped and slid, a comedic sight,
As blossoms flew in pure delight.

I watched in awe as color swirled,
This tiny world so brightly twirled.
And with each laugh, the petals flew,
Time stood still; what else could we do?

A picnic broke out with much fun,
Eating cookies under the sun.
Mom swatted bees; the dog chased flies,
In this bouquet of silly highs.

A Dance of Colors in Stillness

A flower stood beneath the light,
In the breeze, it swayed with delight.
I tried to dance, but tripped instead,
On its roots; I laughed 'til I bled.

A butterfly joined my flailing game,
With wings so bright, it took the fame.
We spun together, colors did clash,
And soon, I found myself in a splash.

The neighbor watched from his old chair,
His eyebrows raised; he couldn't bear.
With every twirl, my shoes flew high,
"Oh dear!" he said, "You'll touch the sky!"

The flowers giggled, oh, what a scene,
A dance of colors, bright and keen.
In the garden of laughter, brave and bold,
The joy of blooms never gets old.

The Heart in a Fragile Blossom

With petals soft as cotton candy,
I spotted something really dandy.
A frog in boots—oh what a sight,
    Sitting pretty in floral light.

He croaked a tune that made me grin,
"Let's dance!" he said, "Come join in."
    A flower cap on his tiny head,
    Had me laughing 'til I begged.

He wiggled, jiggled like a pro,
While trying not to steal the show.
The daisies swayed, the sun, it shone,
In this garden, we felt right at home.

The heart of bloom, a funny plight,
For frogs and me share pure delight.
    Fragile blossoms hold our glee,
    In this whimsical garden spree.

Nature's Tears in Stillness

Tiny drops hang and sway,
Wishing for a sunny day.
A ladybug on a mission,
Sipping dew with great ambition.

A spider's web, a work of art,
Caught a breeze - oh, what a start!
The squirrel stares with big ol' eyes,
As raindrops dance and heaves a sigh.

Each bloom yawns, ready to tease,
Betting on the pollen breeze.
Curious bees buzz about,
Wondering if there's more to scout.

The sun peeks through with a grin,
"It's time to play - let's try again!"
Nature chuckles, and with ease,
Wakes the world from dreams to tease.

Fragments of Color by the Glass

A splash of blue in morning light,
Whispers of red add pure delight.
While yellow giggles in the breeze,
Hoping to tease the bumblebees.

Through the panes, a world so bright,
Purple thinks it's the star tonight.
Green shouts loud, "Don't count me out!"
As they plan their wild spring shout.

Orange laughs, a cheeky hue,
Waving at the clouds so blue.
Each color twirls in joyous dance,
In a game of chance to enhance.

Sunshine spills and splashes wide,
Nature's palette can't be denied.
The colors clash, then harmonize,
With silly grins, they mesmerize.

Remnants of an Unfurling Dawn

A sleepy bloom stirs with a yawn,
Stretching wide at the crack of dawn.
"Is it really time to rise?"
It says while squinting its bright eyes.

Sun beams like a tickling friend,
Chasing shadows 'round the bend.
"Let's wake up!" it sings in glee,
As night retreats — oh, can't you see?

The dew still winks, with dreams so grand,
As if to say, "Just take my hand!"
A flutter here, a shiver there,
Nature's pranks are everywhere!

Laughter fills this blooming space,
Each flower springs to join the race.
In the warmth, they spin and twirl,
As daylight teases the waking world.

Silent Stories of the Greenhouse

Within these walls, a tale unfolds,
Of green shoes and seeds of gold.
Each corner holds a secret cheer,
Whispered in soil — oh, so near.

Tomato plants, a jolly crew,
Debating what they'll grow and chew.
Lettuce dreams of salad fate,
While mint plans how to decorate!

Cacti laugh in prickly tones,
"Can't touch this!" they hum in groans.
As flowers flaunt their colors bright,
Competing for the morning light.

The greenhouse buzzes, a comical show,
Every leaf has a tale to bestow.
In this leafy drama, fun abounds,
As nature whispers all around.

A Journey on the Breeze

A light waft of colors, dancing in the sun,
They flutter and wiggle, oh what fun!
Chasing a neighbor's cat with glee,
Who thinks it's a game, oh silly me!

Whispers of laughter, lost in the air,
Tickling the noses, without a care.
A breeze tickles toes, a giggle brings cheer,
And all the neighbors start to peer!

The fluff of a cloud joins in the jest,
As I trip on a shoe, oh what a test!
The blossoms giggle, the wind gives a shout,
Turns out my hat just blew right out!

But still they swirl, my colorful friends,
A journey on laughter that never ends.
Beneath the sun's glow, in this sweet tease,
We dance together upon the breeze.

The Beauty of Fleeting Moments

A wink from the sun, a peek from the sky,
Squirrels in bow ties, oh my, oh my!
A jump and a twist, a mishap or two,
A dance of the flowers, in shades of blue.

Each tick of the clock, a burst of delight,
As I slip on a puddle, oh what a sight!
Flowers giggle softly, while I do my best,
To juggle a sandwich during this quest.

A hop and a skip, through petals I glide,
While butterflies chuckle, with wings open wide.
Moments are fleeting, like popcorn in air,
I just hope my lunch doesn't end in despair!

Yet here in this chaos, I find my own bliss,
In laughter and missteps, there's nothing amiss.
For the beauty of life, with quirks and with glee,
Is a masterpiece painted, just you wait and see!

Delicate Textures of Time

In the garden of giggles, a tickling breeze,
Laughter unravels like the fluff from the trees.
As I stumble on daisies, the sun holds its breath,
A moment of wonder, a dance with no death.

With friends all around, we frolic and spin,
A tumble, a roll, oh where to begin?
The scent of the laughter, so divine and sweet,
Oh, how we parade on our dance-party feet!

The textures are fine, like laughter's own thread,
As we weave through the blossoms, our hearts full of red.

We slip on some humor, a splash and a giggle,
While serious daisies just watch us and wiggle.

These moments, so fleeting, a comedy show,
In the spectrum of sunlight, our joys overflow.
So let's hold on tight to these delicate days,
Where laughter is woven in oh-so-fun ways!

Blossoms caressed by Silence

In the hush of the morning, a soft little yawn,
The blooms are debating who's prettiest drawn.
With giggles they whisper, a floral debate,
While I chase after bees with a oversized plate.

A waltz of delusions, each blossom a friend,
As I try to dance, unexpected my end!
Overroots and rocks, I tumble and roll,
While the flowers just chuckle, I'm losing control!

In silence they chatter, as I make my stance,
Trying so hard to join in their dance.
But laughter's the rhythm, the tune in the air,
And the best kind of silence is knowing I'm there.

So let's sway with the flowers, and join in the jest,
In this merry circus, where we are all blessed.
Though time may be fleeting, these smiles will stay,
In gardens of giggles where we laugh the day!

www.ingramcontent.com/pod-product-compliance
Lightning Source LLC
Chambersburg PA
CBHW072136070526
44585CB00016B/1709